A NEW BEGINNING

A NEW BEGINNING

A NEW BEGINNING

**BY
VERONICA BROOKS**

ISBN: 0-7392-0160-3

SCRIPTURE TAKEN FROM "KING JAMES" VERSION OF
THE Holy Bible

Printed in the USA by

MORRIS PUBLISHING

3212 East Highway 30 • Kearney, NE 68847 • 1-800-650-7888

TABLE OF CONTENTS

DEDICATION

To the redeemer of my soul, my Lord Jesus Christ who is the one that gave me the knowledge and inspiration to publish poetry He placed in my thoughts. I am only a servant of God, trying to tell any and everybody about my Jesus. Also I dedicate this book to my children, Shaunteh and Courtney (Alex), and in loving memory of my great grand-mother, Beulah Childs-Brooks.

ACKNOWLEDGEMENTS

Pastor Keith Hood, his wife and first lady of Truth and Victory United Pentecostal Church, Mary Hood. My oldest sister Cathy Willingham, and my mother Lelia Brooks-Giles. And thanks to sis, Veronica Colbert for the Art work

EDITORS

Sheri Kimbrough, Cathy Hunter and Terri Lockett my sisters in Christ.

FORWARD

After every trial and tribulation, every "thank you Lord I made it through". After every "whew, that was close" and "Lord you did it again," there was always *A New Beginning*. Every morning when we awake it's *A New Beginning*. This is why we that remain are still here today. Nothing stays the same; neither trouble nor prosperity lasts always. The word of God says, "To everything there is a season and a time..."(Ecclesiates 3:1). No matter how the situation ended, even in death, and eternity there is *A New Beginning*. Not just here on earth, but in the spiritual realm as well, where the physical eye can't always see. Nevertheless there is an end and a beginning of all things except concerning God Almighty. He has always been and will always be.... He has no end and He was here before there was a beginning. (Think about that for a minute).

In this book you will be able to read the writer's thoughts before she was prompted to write the poem that was inspired by God. These poems will uplift your spirit, make you to think, and hopefully make you smile. Some may even make you cry. Hopefully you will enjoy each and every one of them. They may even remind you of your own thoughts or experiences. These poems are not just thoughts, but they are real life situations and experiences that actually happened. So there may be some things in these writings that you may be able to identify with. Maybe the thought itself, or even the poem. However you feel when you read them, I pray that they will open your soul, your mind and your spirit to *A New Beginning* with God.

I DIED AND WAS GOING TO HELL

I died on a clinic table and I heard the doctor say, "we lost her". I started looking around to see what they had lost too. Then it hit me, "hey fool, he's talking about you! I began to look around, as my body was floating past the floor and into the ground. I was conscience and could hear every sound. They were shooting me with so many cc's of this and pumping my heart with that... I said, "come on!" with a loud cry... but no body could hear me... why?

My body, the table, the doctor and nurses had become so small, so far way ....I was now a long ways from the surface of the earth...I was dead! But I knew that I was saved, I had accepted Christ as my personal savior and was living what I thought was a good life.... went to church on Sundays... So why did I hear the wailing and moaning and crying where I was going? Finally I came to the realization, "This is not heaven, I'm going to hell! Oh my God I'm on my way to hell. There was no light in that tunnel, just charcoal, black looking tar like substance. As if it was alive and breathing. Suddenly I heard my baby cry and my body sat up on that same clinic bed. I hadn't heard what the bible said we needed to do to be saved... I was living my Christian life under tradition. I didn't know I had to "repent, be baptized in Jesus name and receive the gift of the Holy Ghost" I didn't have that yet. But God knew that one day I would, and thank God this day I do! He gave me "*A New Beginning*". God gave me a second chance, and He'll do the same for you!

DID I TELL YOU ABOUT THE MAN I MET...?

He told me about some promises that I could get.
He asked me did I know about the Holy Ghost that he sent. And for me to receive it, all I had to do was repent.
He said He used to live here, He had to leave, but that He was coming back again. He showed me some nail prints, in His feet and His hands.
Saying that He took a stripe for any and everything that I could ever go through.
Then He looked into my eyes and said, "and I did it all for you".
DID I TELL YOU ABOUT THE MAN I MET?

He said when He died, He went to hell, and took the keys of death right out of satan's hand.
That He would have the chance to win back every soul that's on sea or land.
He said He paid the price for my sins a long long time ago.
And that this information is right in His Word and it's for everyone to know.
He said He left Peter with the plan of salvation, so we could live with God, and not see damnation.
He said once I repent, I needed to be baptized in His name, to have my sins washed away.
In case I should fall, I shall arise, and in sin I would not stay. He said He would never leave me, never forsake me. But that He would always be there. And to go back on His Word, He would not dare. He said you might not hear from Me from time to time, in fact, you won't see Me at all. Just know that I am there in case you fall.

He said he knew all that I had done and everyplace that I had ever been. He said He's been there from the very beginning, and He'll be there till the end. I thought to myself who could this be, to know so much about me? He answered my thought; (can you imagine?) and said, "I know, because I am God and my name is Jesus".
Then he said that I should say and do everything in **His** name. I'm telling you, right then and there my whole life changed! And then He said that I should worship Him, with my life, and never to be ashamed. He said if I look in his word, his promises were all right there in red, black and white. And all through out my life, he had protected me by grace, and the power of His might.
He was so kind and gentle, I could feel his Holy Power. It was convicting and loving, I repented that very hour. He said he left to go prepare a place in heaven just for me. That's when I made up mind, that where Jesus is... is where I wanna be.
DID I TELL YOU ABOUT THE MAN THAT I MET?

ISN'T IT AMAZING WHAT GOD CAN DO?

It's a joy to be apart of an on-going Holy Ghost filled, victorious praying, divine healing, soul winning, bondage delivering, hand clapping, foot stomping, tongue talking Holy Ghost church!
God endowed the saints with his love
Empowered us with his Holy Spirit from above.
He pulled us out of the pit of sin,
Cleaning us up, me and you
ISN'T IT AMAZING WHAT GOD CAN DO?

Since then, there have been times when we wanted to quit.
Maybe just tired, sometimes even sick
We've had endless, sleepless nights of travailing prayer and supplication hours on end of reading, studying and making preparation... for new babies in Christ, and our own congregation.
This is God's will church, saints we were meant to be.
This is our reasonable service, even when it seems fit for an army—it's just a little from me, and a little from you.
ISN'T IT AMAZING WHAT GOD CAN DO?

He can make our dreams of winning souls reality
The outcome is our big church family.
Look around saints, it's truly worth it all, for us to make a stand, and for us to stand tall.
We've been taught to wave the psalms and the willows... to cross the bayous and the billows.
As a result, we are still here today thank God, Jesus made a way.
We're not making it on our own. We are making it over, because we are resting on God's shoulder.

ISN'T IT AMAZING WHAT GOD CAN DO?

And just think, He's not through!

5

thought…

Sometimes everything you strive for in the Lord, all that you pray for, fast for, is to be closer to the Lord. You push to get in a spiritual realm to envision His face. You want to be in His very existence. You want to be caught up somehow into the very arms of Jesus Christ. You hunger for a certain closeness that no one else can fulfill, and that you never had before. Because sometimes when you prayed, God took you into a Spiritual realm. And it was awesome and you want to go back. So you push through the selfishness, the cares of this world, and all the fleshly desire. Once you go through a couple of levels of prayer you find yourself at a halt, a brick wall. And you're still just not close enough.

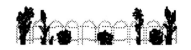

BROKEN HEART

MY HEART IS NOT BROKEN BECAUSE
THE BILLS ARE DUE, NOT EVEN
BECAUSE OF SICKNESS OR PAIN.
MY HEART IS NOT BROKEN BECAUSE
SOMETIMES I FEEL ALL ALONE, AS
THOUGH LIFE HAS NOTHING TO GAIN.
NOT EVEN BECAUSE I FEEL
LIKE I NEED MORE MONEY
OR A NEW JOB. MY HEART IS NOT
BROKEN BECAUSE OF ALL THE
TRIALS AND TRIBULATIONS
THAT I HAVE BEEN THROUGH...
MY HEART IS BROKEN LORD,
BECAUSE I REALLY WANNA BE
CLOSER TO YOU!

Thought.....

Anyone who claims to have a burden to win souls to God, should always pray and seek God's direction in winning souls to the kingdom of God. When you realize who you are praying to, and recognize the awesome God who delivered you then you will know that God himself did and does hear your prayers. Because of your faith and your heart's desire, He will answer your prayers and the answer will be a first class delivery. There are loved ones in your family, co-workers on your job. There are people we run into that are ill, and have physical defects, and we know that God can heal, deliver, and save them. We know this because He has done it for us or for somebody we know. And so, we count on Him to tell us exactly what to say when witnessing. The perfect words to get their attention. After all, God did not save us to be selfish and keep the good news for ourselves....

A SOUL WINNER'S PRAYER

My father in heaven, soul of perfection, spirit of redemption, joy so divine, Lord of Lords and King of Kings, my crucified Christ. Lord give me a hungry person with whom I can share this truth and plan of salvation.... That they may never see the pit of damnation. Grant me the opportunity to give a soul the chance you have given me...whisper to me the words to say to them so that they may hear of thee. Lord open their ears before I get there or they come to me. However you do it, Lord send a soul that I may tell of thee.

A NEW BEGINNING

Many times when you think it's the end it's
just a new beginning
When you think you're fighting a losing
battle you really are winning!
When you need something from God
And you won't let go of what you have that
He may give you more
You wait much longer lack of faith many
times closes an open door
Fear is the opposite of faith doubt produces
continuos failure and discontentment
God is watching and waiting hoping you'll
receive the blessings He already sent
Wake up, smell the coffee
Stand on his word everyday is a new day
When you think it's the end
It's just a new beginning
when you start to pray.

Thought....

God is so awesome, so powerful, and He is omnipotent! I mean He is the supreme Spirit that created the universe. He spoke the world into existence. He set the moon and the stars in place; He actually created and formed you with his Holy hands, He gave you life. He moves clouds, instructs lightening where to strike. He is God almighty. The creator of everything! Knowing this, that when God himself literally breathes His Spirit (His life and power) inside you. And when He have filled you with the Holy Ghost, do you really believe that your body would not have a reaction, a response to such a holy, awesome breath? We have involuntary reactions or responses to viruses, colds and flu. . When we receive a cold virus we respond by sneezing coughing, sniffling chills and fever. When we receive a sudden impact of pain, a sound comes out of our mouth; ouch, maybe a scream. When there's joy; laughter or a smile a chuckle or two. Why wouldn't there be any automatic response of the in-filling of the Holy Spirit. It is an automatic response to speak in a spiritual language when we receive the spiritual breath of God. Just like it happened in the book of Acts to those who received the gift of the Holy Spirit.....

HOLY POWER

When we experience the in-filling of the one and only, Holy, divine, pure, heavenly bound, power over the enemy, spiritual communion, gift of the Lord's Holy breath... coming inside our body, mind, and soul; making eternal life visible and more important than gold. The fibers inside the body, the atoms, and molecules start to change, form and rejuvenate into spiritual cells that enable the stamp of God to be put on our forehead, that only God can see...And when that trumpet sounds, we wont be left here.

Just knowing that Jesus has poured himself literally into our bodies, that we may walk, talk, exhort, teach, pray, witness, love, submit, obey, forgive and live holy every hour. We will worship Him in spirit and truth, when He's filled us with His Holy Power

Thought…..

I was listening to someone, they were complaining about a situation that we were in. I had been in that situation longer than she had been. And when I told her that I had been there for awhile, she said "how have you managed to be in this dreadful place and still be sane?" And I began to think about that…. I thought to myself "that's because I had not been the one that was keeping me. I suddenly realized that because of the goodness of God I was still alive and well, I had given up a long time ago. And when I did He took over…

HOW I MADE IT OVER

There's a song that says; sometimes I wonder how I made it over. And as I sit and think about all the battles I've fought the task came and left so fast, I hardly remember the first from the last. Some came by day, some even on the hour and I only complained. But by his grace, still I was sane. Well it just made me see that the Lord had been taking care of me He washed me when I was dirty, He straightened me up and made me sturdy, He washed my feet and combed my hair, He even took away all my despair. He picked me up when I fell down He lifted my feet off the ground. He soothed my body when I was in pain, He kept me strong, and He kept me sane. He hugged me when I was crying because He knew I was trying. So when I sit down and I wonder how I made I over, it's because the whole time I was resting on God's shoulder!

thought...

We spend so much time worrying and being overly concerned with things that really don't amount to a hill of beans. I mean in the end, the things we put so much emphasis on have very little bearing on the real meaning of life and serving our Lord. I believe if we could hear from somebody, who wasted as much time as we sometimes do, they would have plenty to warn us about. This poem was derived from a sermon preached by Pastor Keith Hood. It was the kind of message you would never forget...

IF GRAVES COULD TALK

There are graves that have different stones--
Some big some small. In them are people who
Died and could take nothing at all
The only thing left was the body, which is now under the grass that
grows. And the soul...who knows, only
If graves could talk –

I'm sure there were some that were rich and some
Even poor but in the grave money have not a
value anymore.
Some were full-grown people and some were just
babies, and then there were men, children, and
ladies. All ages and colors, for in death it doesn't matter, death has
no respect of persons when it does call when the appointed time
has come
No one can escape nor stall, for death watches
For lost souls like a hawk, only

16

If graves could talk
I'm sure there were some that went to heaven
And some to hell only the day of judgement will tell.... Of those
who died and went to hell.
I'm sure they'd like to come to their loved ones
And say, hearken to His call He is drawing you today. He's called
you many times don't you
Remember, this fire burns in hell from January to December
Don't worry about your clothes or even a husband
Or wife, get to know Jesus He is life.
In hell we seek death and death cannot be found
Only burning and wailing and gnashing of teeth
Pain and suffering is never complete. The dreadful thing is, we all
had a choice, but out of rebellion and disobedience we chose this
walk, only
If graves could talk –

We'd tell you don't concern yourselves with fancy
Cars and showcase homes, or even a savings
account. Material things and the cares of the world, all temporal,
have no meaning and no amount.
Don't worry about who's talking about who and
What somebody said – in hell worldly things won't be available to
the dead. Get God in your life, seek salvation with all your heart.
And from God, let nothing keep you apart.
Now that I'm here I wish I could warn just one of you; don't stiff-
arm God let Him do what He wants to do. I tell you my friend this
place called hell there is no end. So while you have breath in your
body and can talk and walk. Get to know Jesus that's what I'd tell
you only
If graves could talk –

Thought.....
While sitting, and resting enjoying the
midday. I could feel the presence of the Lord.
Pondering on the words that my pastor
preached, I began to build a fire. When the fire
started to die, I'd add more wood, this time I
really put a lot of wood, and suddenly I heard
a winded noise, and I turned to the fireplace
and the blaze was high and full of power! I
suddenly remembered reading about the first
outpouring of the Holy Ghost. I remembered
the scripture saying" suddenly there came a
sound from heaven as of a rushing mighty
wind, and it filled all the house where they
were sitting. And there appeared unto them
cloven tongues like as of fire, and it sat upon
each of them. And they were all filled with the
Holy Ghost, and began to speak with other
tongues, as the Spirit gave the utterance." And
I took a double look at the fire in my fireplace,
and realized that Luke was describing a real
fire, only in the spiritual sense. Because in
that fireplace was a sound of a rushing mighty
wind, and that fire was consuming everything
in that fire place, just like on the day of
Pentecost the Holy fire of God came down and
consumed all that were sitting in the upper
room.
Folks the Holy Ghost is just as real today as it
was on the first day it was poured out....

FIRE, FIRE, LIKE AS OF FIRE

The Holy Ghost came in like a rushing mighty
wind
It was Jesus, the comforter, that He promised
to send
And all who were in the upper room by His
Spirit they were consumed. Their souls
renewed as the Holy Ghost came in.
And just think, it happens today just like back
then.
He fills us with His Holy power, I'm glad to be
In Him, in this day and hour.
He said He'd never leave me
And I know He does not change He's the same
yesterday, Today and forever.
I'm glad I have the promise for He and I to be
together. Just like back then....
Fire, fire, like as of fire the Holy Ghost came
in like a rushing mighty wind....

Thought..
There are days when
you are just restless,
and can't seem to do
enough for God. You've
been praying, fasting,
witnessing and giving.
There is still something
missing. Where is God?
You have to slow down
sometimes and wait to
hear from Him.
Sometimes we get in a
hurry and we want
things to happen right
then. But God has the
perfect time and place.
We need to do our
part, the basics. The
hardest part of the
basics is waiting on
God. We are not with
God, He is with us....

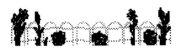

I'M GLAD YOU'RE WITH ME LORD, LET'S GO!

Oh how glad my heart is, to serve you Lord,
and only you; to do all that you command me
to do. And if I fall short Lord, and I know that
sometimes I will, quicken my spirit to wait on
you and tell me to be still. Then I can say" I'm
glad you're with me Lord, let's go!"

And while you lead, I will follow, taking one
step at a time, not worrying about tomorrow
when you exhale, I will inhale....and when you
say, "how are we doing saint? I'll say "doing
well"
I'm glad you're with me Lord let's go!

When you lay me down, I'll sleep. When I
sleep, I'll see your visions and dreams. When
you awaken me, I'll know what you want me to
pray, and as I begin to pray, I'll see you move
(in the spirit). Then and only then will I say,
"I'm glad you're with me Lord, let's go!

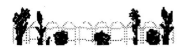

Thought....
So many times I want to do God's will. But
I don't always know what that is, that's
why I just want to turn it all over to Him,
so He can just do whatever He wants.

LORD HOW DO YOU WANT TO USE ME

Father in heaven as I pray. I give myself unto you
Lord have your way and do what you want to do
I give unto you this heart (which is the mind) to
think your thoughts and to do your will
To control this body, whether to move or to be still
LORD HOW DO YOU WANT TO USE ME

I give unto you these hands that you may touch
all that you desire. That you may go about healing
And casting out, with your Holy Ghost fire
Lord I give unto you these feet, that you may walk
As you please. That there be no mischief in these
steps that you may walk with ease
LORD HOW DO YOU WANT TO USE ME

And unto you Lord, everything that is part of this old
wretched body. I give unto you, Lock, stock, and
barrel. You are the potter; I'm the clay. This body
will only do what you will and what you say.
LORD HOW DO YOU WANT TO USE ME?

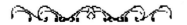

Thought...
Have you ever made a promise to God
and suddenly realized that you slipped
away from that promise, or deviated a
little? I told God how I wanted to be
used by Him and allow Him to control
my life. And I was sincere and honest
too. Then the next thing I knew I was
trying to do my own thing and the Holy
Spirit reminded me of that promise...

LORD TEACH ME TO DO WHAT MY LIPS PROMISED TO YOU!

Now that I've given all my members unto you
Why am I still trying to do what I want to do?
**LORD TEACH ME TO DO WHAT MY LIPS
PROMISED TO YOU!**

Search my mind oh Lord and find sincerity in there
I cannot take back what I've given unto you. A broken-
promise, this I cannot bear.
Teach me, oh Lord to leave that which I have given;
For it is because of your grace... that I am still living.
**LORD TEACH ME TO DO WHAT MY LIPS
PROMISED TO YOU!**

For it is by your grace and your mercy that I see each
day;
Help me to hide your word in my heart that I may know
the way.
For mine heart is desperately wicked,
Only you know what I will and won't do; So..
**LORD TEACH ME TO DO WHAT MY LIPS
PROMISED TO YOU.**

Thought....
Sometimes you have those days where you
think; now I know God is still God no matter
what I'm going through. I've been through
enough already to know a better day is gonna
come. And you try to encourage yourself and
talk yourself into a good attitude and a
positive way of looking at the situation. And
then you finally say "God this is not working",
and you desperately need to hear from the
Lord. And you will....

LORD I NEED TO HEAR FROM YOU

Lord, you've been with me for a
very long time,
Since I can remember; through
The good and the bad from January to December.
All the prayers you have heard
I thank you Lord for listening to every word. I've
prayed in different rooms, behind bars and free,
every single time Lord, you knew that it was me.
I've prayed when I was cold, even in the heat;
when I was full of energy and sometimes beat. I've
prayed in the snow, and in the rain. When I felt
good, even when I was in pain. I prayed when I
was sick and couldn't lift mine own head.
I realize Lord, even in the deeps of despair you
have always been there.
So in those times, I had a broken heart,
Felt like I was falling apart. You reminded me, of
all that you brought me through. And that's why
Lord, I always need to hear from you.

27

Thought...

*He's worthy to be praised whether we
feel like it or not. No matter what is
going on in your life and what is not. It
is imperative that we do not allow the
enemy to steal our praise. No matter
what is right or what is wrong. In our
life God is still on the throne, and He is
still God almighty. Count your blessings
and not your troubles...*

PRAISING HIM MORNING, NOON, AND NIGHT

My early morning praise unto the Lord He fights all my
battles with His holy sword. Oh how I love just hearing His
name since I have met Jesus, nothing in my life is the same.
The undying love that He has for me
Fills my mind all the day giving
Praises to thee. In the noonday when I'm thinking of all the
things that He does, Lord I know all good things
Come directly from you above.
Late in the evening, when I'm
Exhausted from the fiery darts of the day; I'm glad to go
home so that I can really pray.
Oh Lord, how I love to praise your name; since I met you,
my life is not the same. Late at night when the whole house
is asleep I feel your presence, as I
begin to weep. Oh how He ministers
to my soul; all the hidden sorrows and cries, only He can
unfold. He is the deliverer of my soul
Oh how I love to praise
you Lord, so that you are never out
of my sight. And that's why I'm praising
you Lord morning, noon, and night.

29

(This poem was derived from a sermon preached by a visiting evangelist, Brother Granger.) You may have a degree in a category or two. You may have an I.Q. that is the highest in the land. Education is good when you recognize the source from which knowledge comes. Just remember there is a master of all and His knowledge is the full capacity of the word. And no one on this earth or in heaven can outsmart, out think, or even out create the knowledge and wisdom of God....

THE HIGHEST EDUCATION

God has the highest education
And He's not into creed or denomination
His credentials are in the word
It's called the Holy Bible.
He made the heavens and the earth too
He put the bass in the thunder, and
Breath in me and you.
He put green on the grass
And the blue in the sky;
For us to enjoy and lift His
Name up high
His degrees are all to the fullest
Capacity, He's the master in physics, astronomy
Medicine, even physiology in everything
He has a degree. He is a counselor
He's wonderful and anything we could ever
Need is in Him. He holds the key
And His charge to us, is this, all of
His services are free

Thought.....

*It's a blessing to see each and everyday.
With the trials and tribulations of life, we
need to always thank God because
tomorrow is not promised to us. We spend
too much time complaining and talking
about what's not right. We need to just
take one day at a time...*

ONE MORE DAY

*When I woke up this morning I thought "Whew, Lord you
brought me through it, one more day." I wonder if anyone
else wakes up feeling this way. Yesterday was bad, I thought
on everything that was wrong; each problem, I thought it
through, hard and long...until finally, I saw no break;
Resolution seemed too far-fetched and far too late. I
remembered that I went through this same feeling and
dilemma once before. But one day I looked around, I didn't
have that same problem anymore. I thought to myself, God's
been good and He's brought me out many times from the
very worst. Just when I thought I couldn't make it through;
before long.... One was gone, and sooner or later came a
new! But what I realized is this.... That one by one they
came and they left. Each morning I woke to a new day, a
new breath. So now, when I wake up in the morning, with
thanksgiving in every way... I say to the Lord, "Whew, Lord
you brought me through it, one more day."*

SIN

What is this thing called sin, that consumes the spirit and causes damnation and pain; causes strife, jealousy, and produce words to be vain......
This sin is of the flesh and drives the body into temptation, condemnation, deliberation and most of all failure and disappointment that will send you straight to hell; here's the story, listen as I tell... flesh is sinful and contrary to God.
As I look through the very skin that covers me; I realize there is more than meets the eye... the soul still exists even when the flesh die.
That there will be consequences too horrible to even entertain, because of sin and that self glory oh, so vain. Perhaps we don't realize that even when we are killed and buried, the mind, which is the soul, lives on....
The thing that is left to torture will be the soul, the rest is gone...there will be memories of pain and heat and cold and frustration, hatred and doubt, sorrow and condemnation...why? You ask and I'll tell you this day... that while you have breath take heed to what I say. The bible didn't lie when Peter stood up and said "be baptized everyone of you in the name of Jesus Christ". He did not say that Father, Son and Holy Ghost (His titles) would suffice.
The reason is that the name would remit the sins and wash them away. Why would things be any different today, the bible says He's the same yesterday, today and forever. When He said repent, that's just what He meant. And "ye shall receive the gift of the Holy Ghost" which do you believe the most? your tradition or what the bible said.... It's the difference between heaven and hell
And why don't we believe acts 2:39...I hope you make it yours, cause I made it mine. "For the promise is unto you, and to your children, and to all that are afar off.... (Do you think you were ever afar off, from God?)..Even as many as the Lord God shall call." if you left this one promise and refuse to make it your own...you believed none of the bible...and when the trumpet sounds............you'll be left alone.

34

WHO IS THAT SOMEONE

When you wake up in the morning and you see the morning light there's a special someone that brought you through the night. When you are in trouble and you need a friend, someone will be there to hold your hand. When it seems like all odds are against you and you can't see your way through, I know a someone that will be there for you. When you are tired and you have to run cause you just cannot be late, someone will be there to hold open the gate. And when you stop and realize all your battles were fought with the greatest sword you will see that, that someone is the Lord.

WHO IS GOD? (1)
He stretched His hand and made the earth
He formed man straight from the dirt
He breathed into His nostrils and gave him life
He took a rib and formed his wife
He poured out rain to cover all that the heavens could see.
Calling out Noah and his family.
He even parted the waters called the Red Sea
WHO IS GOD?

He opened Rebecca's womb and gave her a child promised
nations to the seed of Abraham for a while
He quickened Samuel and gave him strength
He put water in a jawbone by the Holy Spirit
And Mary's womb, He put Himself in it.
WHO IS GOD?

He can make the skies, clear, black or blue
The sun shines when He commands it to
Even the donkey talked when He told it to
He put green in the grass, blue in the sky.
WHO IS GOD?

Bushes burned and never consumed
King Solomon's dress couldn't compare
To the flowers God has bloomed.
He went to hell in a mass of power
While satan still tremble this very hour.
He snatched the keys right out of His hand
Robbed Himself in flesh and became a man.
WHO IS GOD?

WHO IS GOD (2)

He laid the foundations of the earth, and the measures thereof commanding the morning from the night created the heavens above. He knows the depth of the sea discerns the bone from the marrow in you and me.

WHO IS GOD?

He knows the gateway to hell and hath delivered and have conquered death He numbered the hairs on our head, even measures our every breath.
He gives life to our mortal bodies and understanding to our heart commands the snowflake to form, and direct the dewdrops where to start.

WHO IS GOD?

He feed the wild beast in places no man has ever, and will ever go while death follows our feet, like a shadow, moving fast, thank God He is patient, and His anger slow.
We are as sheep to the slaughter, and know not the fiery darts of the day but God is a light unto our feet as He directs our pathway.

WHO IS GOD?

His love causes conviction upon our hearts, we are baptized in His name. That is "Jesus Christ," and filled with His Holy Spirit not only that we might be saved, but to bring someone else in it!
That we all may have life more abundantly and joy forever more He is the God of our salvation, He is the key to a used to be locked door.

37

Thought...
If you ever get to a place where you feel like you are tired of praying, tired of seeking God and tired of being obedient to the word of God and you have stopped praying. This is a sure sign of a backslider. The enemy knows that if he can just get you to slowly slack up on that prayer, and stop talking to God so much, he's gotcha. Anytime you stop talking to someone you no longer have a relationship with them Think about when you don't want to deal with somebody, or decide you no longer want to be in their presence and you stop talking to them. Concerning the Lord, you don't just stop praying suddenly. But the prayers just seem to get shorter and shorter each time. And you finally get to a place where you just don't have the time. And the devil does not want you to know what he is doing. So he moves slowly, turning up the heat with each step....

ﾔﾔﾔﾔﾔ

ALWAYS PRAY

My heart was heavy, as I crawled to my closet to pray;
I said to myself, why does this seem so hard, I do this
everyday.
For every prayer I had to push to pray each and every
time. In fact, sometimes I felt like I was losing my
mind. Some things had changed, but still too much was
the same;
Because I was still trying to do my own thing...
Some days I look ahead, and life seemed worthless, and
I wanted to die
Other day's life was awesome, even then I questioned
why.
When I look back and remembered all the darkness
that used to surround me;
I said, " oh Lord, I am thankful, for the goodness of
thee"
And his reply was " out of all that I have brought you
through you're still doing what you want to do.
Because of rebellion,
And disobedience, sin got in the way.
I'm glad for your sake that you still pray.
satan desires to sift you like wheat, he wants you long
gone.
But because of prayer... I've allowed you to live on".

Thought....

You know many times we call ourselves soul winners and witnesses of God. But when things don't go the way we think they should. When people don't respond the way we want them to, we become impatient, and are ready to give up. Instead, we need to persevere, press on, keep planting seeds, and keep reaching out to people who are not saved. After all, there are more sinners than there are saved folk. Don't you know we got a long way to go, and a lot of territory to cover? It should not matter if they are old or young, rich or poor, black or white. If you are truly a soul winner you will talk to anybody about the love of God and the plan of salvation...

ARE YOU A SOWER?

Know this, I say and know it well
That a sower always has a story to tell
A sower testifies wherever he or she may go
A sower will learn the word and scripture they know. As we
plant and go about we go in faith without a doubt
And as we sow, this is what we are to expect
Some fell by the wayside and the fowls devoured them up
Some fell in stony places where they
had not much earth. Because they had no root, the sun
scorched and burned them up. Some fell among thorns and the
thorns sprung up and choked them.
All these that are above can be very few
For it's numbers warfare and much depends on you.
Now when you sow each day to as many as you cross
With a kind word or a warm smile. Maybe a pat on the back.
Then with faith and prayer they will begin to grow --- and
those are the ones that fell into good ground and brought forth
fruit; and some a hundred fold, some sixty fold, some thirty
fold, they all followed suit.
Are you a sower?

 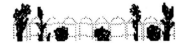

Thought....

When you sit under a preacher that preaches the un-cut, unadulterated word of God, you can believe you are going to be cut up, kicked in the face, stomped to the ground, put in a head lock, and a choke hold. You will be beat down to a weeping bag of dirt. Why? Because the word of God is alive. And the truth gets down to where you are living. " The word of God is quick, and powerful, and sharper than any two-edged sword, piercing even to the dividing asunder of the soul and spirit, and of the joints and the marrow, and is a discerner of the thoughts and the intents of the heart. (Hebrews 4; 12) And when hearing the word of God can do all that to you, I guarantee you won't be able to say "he's not talking to me, I'm doing everything right." You will be broken into pieces but you will be put back together again. And it will be worth it all when we stand before God and He welcomes us into the heavenly kingdom...

PREACHER, PREACH TO ME

I came to church one day; I went back again that night, I felt a spirit of conviction because I knew my life wasn't right. The word of God opened my eyes and I finally saw the light. I shouted, Preacher, Preach to me. I went back, week after week. And years had gone by; He preached continuing in truth, not a single word a lie. He preached against fornication and gossiping and hate, he preached "come to prayer on time and don't you ever be late". He preached love, jealousy, lasciviousness, and pain; I sat there SHOUTING "amen" and "oh me", every word I understood and clearly I could see. I shouted Preacher, Preach to me. I heard him loud and clear; the words just seemed to ring in my ear. I wanted to hear every word, good or bad I needed to be there as long as he preached the truth, I didn't care. Even when I went home and tried to sleep at night; I could hear that preacher preaching, I knew he was preaching right. Straight down the line he preached, and he never backed up. He didn't put up, nor shut up, he just preached. And every time he preached there was always something that pertained to me. And I shouted, preacher come on now… preacher, preach to me.

43

SAINTS THAT AIN'T

We see people claiming a walk, a talk with God.
Saints worshipping, praying, running, and giving
Him all the praise; but there are some pretending,
sinning, faking, and going through the motions for
months, weeks and days.

We hear conversations of saints saying what I would
and would not do; when we see the real person,
your very own words are making a liar out of you.
Picking and pointing fingers, at one another; no
true concern or love for our sister or brother.

How can we worship in spirit and truth, when we
are too busy to support our own youth? We go
about as a "know it all", trying to tell others how
to worship and pray; giving our own interpretation
of what the pastor preached today.

What about you, "it's me, it's me, it's me oh Lord,
standing in the need of prayer;
God is the one watching each and every one of us,
he knows, whether we are really here, or there.

SAINTS THAT AIN'T... (Cont.)

We say we want revival, yet we are still in denial.
We say we want new comers filled with the Holy
Ghost, and to be baptized; yet we get them off by
themselves, gossiping and telling lies.

Our concern is not with the word of God and what
He wants us to do; while being a busy body,
wondering who's doing what, and the problem, is
really you. Who are you to tell people what to do?
Have you died, gone to heaven, and come back too!

Jesus is the reason that we live; it's all about Him.
We need to be about our Father's business and not
about someone else's, or even our own;
God's not going to stand for mess, and if we keep it
up, we're gonna be gone! (And it won't be heaven)

Thought...

I was sitting at work one day and I thought to myself, I really don't want to be here. I had so much to do, for the kingdom of God. There were people I needed to try to reach. I wanted to invite them to church. I had bible studies to set up. I had a poem or two I had been working on. I needed more time to pray, more time to seek God. And I was stuck there at work. I thought about the fact that I just needed to quit and go to work for God fulltime. I wanted to be an employee for Jesus Christ....

JESUS CHRIST INCORPORATED

When you fill out the application,
You will need to repent, be baptized in the name of Jesus Christ
for the remission of your sins, and ye shall receive the gift of the
Holy Ghost, you are now a welcomed employee of Jesus Christ
incorporated,
We do what the bible says
As we live this sanctified life.
Jesus himself will direct us,
On how to market for other applicants,
To win souls one by one; we cannot quit
His work must be done.
We must clock in on time
On whatever schedules or shift He has
Placed each of us on; with prayer, and
Supplication without ceasing, until each
And every soul He has called is won.
We must work diligently, seeking His
Word and taking care of our
Responsibilities working spiritually
Using His time smart and wisely. We are now
Employees of Jesus Christ incorporated.

Jesus Christ Inc...(cont.)

Regardless of who we work for, we have to work
whether our employer is God or satan
(one or the other, which ever you allow will
have authority over you)
We do have a choice, and we need to choose God.
we need to touch Him daily, and be
wall to wall filled with His Spirit. His benefits are
awesome and He have a great retirement plan
Crowns and streets of gold in a heavenly land
I'm telling you the benefit package is out of this world.
Now when we punch out and lay down to sleep
we are always on call , for we are His precious sheep.
We sleep in peace, with our minds
At ease and fixed on His kingdom
We awake fresh and ready, clocking in
With prayer, because everywhere we go
We want Jesus, the owner to be there.
He orders our steps at His
Assigned pace. We really believe you're
Going to love this place.
We are glad to have you, we are
One in the body of Christ. By our bodies
Our souls, and even mentally
After all this job is our life
We are preparing for heaven, our eternity.
For we are employees of Jesus Christ incorporated.

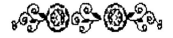

Thought....
Some people walk around like they have the world by the tail. They think they can do what they want when, and how they want to. They are too arrogant to realize you belong either to God or the devil. You're Not really doing your own thing anyway! You are influenced and controlled by your chosen spiritual leader and it's not you. It's either God or the devil. You are gonna serve one of them whether you like it or not. The awesome thing about being a slave to Jesus is that with Him you really are free...

THIS IS WHAT IT IS TO BE FREE..

To be baptized in the Holy Ghost, and in Jesus' name; to know that my old ways of walking, and talking are no longer the same.

To be endued with power from on high; to know that the God I serve is from heaven, high above the sky. To keep my head lifted up looking for Him to come any day or night, and get me.

THIS IS WHAT IT IS TO BE FREE
To be loved by Him that created the earth; to give up the world to praise Him daily, for all that He is worth. To have life, more abundantly. To be free indeed...from the bondage of sin. And to look to Him daily for my every need.

THIS IS WHAT IT IS TO BE FREE

To have truth, and victory, in everything I say and do; to worship Jesus, count on Him and trust in Him too. To love Him with all of my heart and not to worry or care; but to touch Him and know, that I know..., that He is always there.

THIS IS WHAT IT IS TO BE FREE!!

WHAT'S RIGHT AND WHAT'S WRONG?

Sometimes you just don't know
What's right and what's wrong. After you sit
down and reason with yourself and try to figure
out what to do, you're still clueless because it
can't be right and wrong too.

You try to pray, but words seem to
get in your way, or better yet your mind just
goes blank. You struggle with words to say, you
stop and think...if only feelings instead of words
could go up in prayer, instead of words that just
aren't there. Feelings of pain, insecurities,
distrust and doubt. Feelings that we can
sometimes do without.

Some rights and wrongs are obvious
and some you learn through trial and error. And
the ones that you just don't know.... Where do
those wrong and rights go?

To the perplexed and mixed feelings
category and such? The ones that only Jesus can
touch. So if you find yourself wondering and
pondering on what's wrong and what's right to
do
Take it to the Lord, I already know He's the one
that can help you.

YOUR GRACE AND MERCY

Lord, thank you for your grace and mercy, you woke me up this morning you loaned me limbs that I may walk; you opened my mouth that I may talk...Lord you loaned me water to wash my face. You are the one who provided this place. Lord you drove my car controlled the wheels, kept other cars from running into me...God almighty I thank thee. Lord you are so good..... All the things we take for granted time after time...not realizing it's you who is keeping us day by day...

How can anyone think, that its any other way...but they do. They think they are here to stay, and to leave only when they say die...they think they can live how they want and no one can ask them why. They believe that material fortune tells them they are saved, they believe that no man on earth or God in heaven can make them behave....

And I sit back, look and say "Oh Lord, I don't want to be that way.... I want them to know the author and the finisher of my faith. And that is because there was a beginning there is an end... because there is righteousness, there is also sin.... And to know that there is a master of all the heavens and the earth. An almighty God who loves and cares...there is also a deceiver, a roaring lion who seeks to devour and lay snares but your grace and mercy...has kept us even unto this day...your grace and your mercy...thank you Lord, for loving us your way.

51

Thought...
When you feel like you can't make it through and all odds are against you, there is always a Miracle around the corner, if you have hope. Hope can keep you holding on when you have lost faith. Sometimes the situation will seem so bad.

Some how you allowed the enemy to rob you of your faith. But.... If the faith has left and you look around and you are still alive, you're still breathing.... There is hope. Hold on to hope and don't ever let go. Cause if you do, your chances will seem slim to none, and life will seem useless....

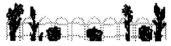

HOPE

What is hope, and can I live without it? The answer is no, I seriously doubt it. When you choose to believe negative reports and doubt just won't do; you are trusting in Jesus, and not accepting the hand that this world is trying to deal you.. Life can kill you before you're even dead...that's right my friend, did you hear what I said. You really don't know, if you will make it to heaven or not; you are not there yet, have you forgot? But if you read the promises of God and do what the word says to do.... The word can and will save you. You hope daily to walk and talk right and that you live the word day and night. You hope that you remember to read your bible and help others along the way...hey, you never know, this could be the day. But even if it is, the very day you meet your maker, hope that you make it, pray, that it's so... because without hope you died long ago...

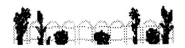

Thought...

As I look around and see the growth of the church, I can see a vision of a very large building filled with saints who have come together to worship God almighty. Loving the sinners, welcoming the visitors, helping them find their way to God, Lives changing. Watching God's church grow...

THE CHURCH PERISH WITHOUT A VISION

Envision in your mind the face of the Lord; even His body down to his feet. Envision His power moving all about en vision His grace and the mercy seat. Envision His protection upon your household envision His goodness, it's forever old. Envision His power and Spirit moving on souls
You have prayed, and supplicated for.
Envision each one of them walking through
Truth's opened door. Envision each of them, receiving the word and beginning to repent
Envision them filled with the Holy Ghost
For which he has sent. Envision them going to
The altar in Jesus name being baptized sins washed away, all hatred, envy, lust, and lies. Envision the angels rejoicing such as they should oh taste and see that the Lord he is good.
The church perish without a vision!

I NEED TO PRAY

*Early in the morning, just before dawn; my
body seems restless, as I start to yawn.*

*I hear the Holy Spirit, calling my name.
" Come talk to me, keep your spirit holy,
that it may never change."*

*I pull myself out of bed, as I begin to
pray; Feeling tired, knowing that my flesh
wants to have its way.*

*And as I pray, I know that the anointing is
covering me; I remember His word, as He
reveals to me.*

*Stand firm, and be thou not removed; seek
my face daily. And you will never lose.*

*Then I start to feel His strength and rest
in the Holy Spirit; and I began to thank
God that He is the one that called me in
it!*

Too Tired?

One cannot imagine an apostolic Holy Ghost filled baptized in
Jesus name saint depressed.
How about one suppressed, pushed down and just a mess!

Too tired to keep living, and too afraid to die.

Eyes weary of crying, and heart too tired to even beat.
The soul seems useless, literally falling from that heavenly seat.

Some days are bearable—others can't even get a prayer through
You wonder if God is really there and is He even listening to you

Too tired to keep living and too afraid to die.

Tired of sickness, pain and things that are tearing your body down
The prayers of faith seems useless and you're only complaining,
when others do come around

No-one to talk to, too tired of singing the blues
Your steps are slothful and you walk like you're wearing two left
shoes

Too tired to keep living and too afraid to die.

It's time for a fight.... the good fight of faith, It's time to survive,
It's time to fast, time to pray.... and it's time to start today.

Have you ever felt like your day was worthless, and you could not
wait for it to be over?
And then tomorrow came and it was a new and great day!

There is hope for tomorrow and if the Lord tarries, it can and will
be a better day
All you have to do is pray....

A Mother's Memorial Prayer

Lord, when you wake me up and I began to pray. Place in my heart a burden for the children of today. Show me what they need and how best to help them along.
Place in their hearts a happy and joyful song.
And sometimes when they start to feel sad or blue...Lord use me to tell them about real love that only comes from you. Now if they begin to worry and can't see their way through. Call on me Lord, and tell me how to reach them for you. But most of all lord.... Help me to do, what I am asking of you.

AUTHOR

Veronica Brooks who's currently residing in the suburbs of Atlanta, Georgia working as a medical insurance biller/bill collector has a true gift of writing poetry. She's been writing poetry since the age of nine. She was born in a small military town near Macon, Georgia called Warner Robins. With Veronica's stepfather being a service man in the airforce, she traveled beginning at the age of four moving from state to state, including overseas. Because of this she experienced a lot of things and found just about everything to write about. It was not until she was born again that she realized why she went through all those trials and tribulations-- to share with others. People often ask, "How do you write like that"? Her reply is simple, "While in prayer, God gives me a title or a sentence and the rest just flows". Veronica thanks God and gives Him all the glory and honor for this heaven sent talent.

Veronica is a single-parent of two, Shaunteh and Courtney. They all attend Truth and Victory United Pentecostal Church in Atlanta, Georgia under the leadership of Pastor Keith Hood. She is very active in her church and has been for the past four years. She thanks God for her children and the church that helped motivate her in writing *A New Beginning*. Everyone who reads *A New Beginning* will probably be able to identify with these writings. These poems express openly and candidly situations and experiences in our normal everyday living. She is able to capture her daily adventure and experiences in words that reach out and touch the soul. You can feel the realism and will be touched intimately as you read each one. To order a copy of *A New Beginning,* please call the number inside the book. Thank You.

To order Additional Copies of *A NEW BEGINNING*, please call 770-300-0497 OR 770-597-0964. Or you may fill out the form below and mail in your order.

Ship to: (please print)

Name_____

Address_____

City, State, _____

Day phone_____

Night phone_____

_____Copies of A *New Beginning* @ 10.00ea $_____

_____ Postage and handling @ 15% per book $_____

Make checks or money orders payable to:

VERONICA BROOKS
3517 B PEACHTREE CORNERS CIRCLE
NORCROSS GA. 30092